31 Days of Prophetic Encouragement for the Weary Warrior

31 Days of Prophetic Encouragement for the Weary Warrior

Alexandria Blackburn

Alexandria Blackburn

First Printing, 2023

Contents

To my precious daughter, Maliyah. May you remain encouraged and strengthened through all life's circumstances, knowing that the Lord has good plans in store for you and a glorious inheritance promised to you!

Love, Mom

Introduction

This book has been placed into your hands as a love letter from your Father to let you know that **He has seen you**! He has seen the long and arduous journey you have walked with Him all these years. He has heard every prayer you've cried out to Him asking Him for things to change. He has been with you every single step of the way. And He has a message of hope that He wants to bring you today! **You have not been forgotten!** He is bringing you new strength!!!

You are not forgotten, for you have been chosen and destined by Father God. The Holy Spirit has set you apart to be God's holy ones, obedient followers of Jesus Christ who have been gloriously sprinkled with his blood. May God's delightful grace and peace cascade over you many times over!
1 Peter 1:2

I wrote this book and these poems after enduring three long years of suffering with the Lord. I was at a point in my life where I had become so beaten down by life's circumstances that I was beginning to feel numb, empty, and lifeless. Maybe that's how you feel right now...

But I began to feel the Lord nudge me to begin writing these poems because I knew He wanted to bring my heart healing through them. Not only did he want to bring my heart healing, but He wanted to use these poems to bring healing to the many other warriors of God out there who had been feeling weak and weary and were in need of new strength!

When we've made a decision to travel the narrow path with the Lord, we have also made the decision to become warriors for the Lord. With the life of a warrior comes intense training! Many times it will feel like the training is there to crush us and kill us, but it's actually all a part of God's plan to forge us into His strong, unstoppable, and immovable warriors! Although it hasn't looked like it, these battles you've been facing are what the Lord has been using to BUILD YOU.

For I know the plans I have for you, declares the Lord, plans for welfare and not for evil, to give you a future and a hope.
Jeremiah 29:11

Let this book be a message to you, that there is life after death! We know the truth of that statement because when Jesus died for us, He resurrected into a glorified body! The Lord is wanting to bring resurrection to every dead place in your life! Every area where you currently feel lifeless and have given up hope, the Lord has promised you resurrection and NEW LIFE!

It's not too good to be true, **IT IS TRUE.**

You have turned my mourning into joyful dancing. You have taken away my clothes of mourning and clothed me with joy, that I might sing praises to you and not be silent. O LORD my God, I will give you thanks forever!
Psalm 30:11-12

But we have this treasure in jars of clay to show that this all-surpassing power is from God and not from us. We are hard pressed on every side, but not crushed; perplexed, but not in despair; persecuted, but not abandoned; struck down, but not destroyed. We always carry around in our body the death of Jesus, so that the life of Jesus may also be revealed in our body. For we who are alive are always being given over to death for Jesus' sake, so that his life may also be revealed in our mortal body. So then, death is at work in us, but life is at work in you.
2 Corinthians 4:7-12

There is power in the blood! When Jesus's blood was poured out on the cross and His body was broken for us, that sealed the promise of new life for those of us who believe! The power of ressurection life lives inside of us when we believe! It's His blood and His body, that remind us of the inheritance that is promised to us! It's His blood and His body that speak a better word over us. It's His blood and His body that give us total freedom from all the things of this world and anything that would try to keep us bound!

And to Jesus, the mediator of a new covenant, and to the sprinkled blood, which says better things than the blood of Abel.

Hebrews 12:24

I feel that the Lord wants to use these truths to set you free from the weariness you've experienced for years now! **As you read this book daily, take communion with the Lord.** Meditate on His body being broken for you, and His blood being poured out for you in order to have a forever relationship with you and give you His Kingdom. Journal your time with the Lord these next 31 days and watch and see how the Lord refreshes your soul and restores your broken heart! I truly believe the Lord will use this intimate time between you and Him to give you new strength and new joy!

But they that wait upon the Lord shall renew their strength; they shall mount up with wings as eagles; they shall run, and not be weary; and they shall walk, and not faint.
Isaiah 40:31

Dear Warrior of God,

Life will come with many sorrows, many battles, and many tests. But there are also times of joy, laughter, love, and peace! No matter what circumstances you endure, remember this scripture:

Finally, be strong in the Lord and in his mighty power. Put on the full armor of God, so that you can take your stand against the devil's schemes. For our struggle is not against flesh and blood, but against the rulers, against the authorities, against the powers of this dark world and against the spiritual forces of evil in the heavenly realms. Therefore put on the full armor of God, so that when the day of evil comes, you may be able to stand your ground, and after you have done everything, to stand. Stand firm then, with the belt of truth buckled around your waist, with the breastplate of righteousness in place, and with your feet fitted with the readiness that comes from the gospel of peace. In addition to all this, take up the shield of faith, with which you can extinguish all the flaming arrows of the evil one. Take the helmet of salvation and the sword of the Spirit, which is the word of God.

And pray in the Spirit on all occasions with all kinds of prayers and requests. With this in mind, be alert and always keep on praying for all the Lord's people.

Ephesians 6:10-18

Love your sister in Christ,
Alex

Day 1

Arise Wounded One

Arise from the dust wounded one.
The Repairer of Brokenness is here.
I know the road you've traveled has been long.
But my presence has always been near.
I've watched you as you've bowed your head
and cried out for my help.
I've seen the tears you've shed and the days you've been filled with doubt.
I've heard the anger in your voice when you told me "enough was enough."
And I've seen the pain in your face, when the going only got more tough.

I know it hasn't been easy and many times you've asked me why.

You've been hopeful for a breakthrough but instead, continuously watched everything die.
You've wondered when life would enter into every dry and barren place.
You've tried your hardest to hold on, even when it no longer felt safe.

But see...
you've always been safe with me.
Even when you didn't feel it.
I had to teach you to trust me, even when you couldn't see it.
I've been forging you into a warrior...that's mighty and unable to be shaken.
I've been producing a substance within you, and that substance only comes from breaking.

You didn't understand then, but now you're about to see...
I had to break you...
So you could start to look more like me.

So lift your head my chosen one.
And dry your eyes.
I'm doing something you've never seen before...
and it's finally time.
Arise from the dust...stand tall. And shake off the past.
The Repairer of Brokenness is here...
and this time, will be nothing like the last!

I know how hard it can be to believe again. When you've experienced so many moments of having deep hope and faith for circumstances to change, but you keep seeing every hope and desire get crushed. I know what it's like to wait for years and years and see nothing change. But I want to encourage you today to increase your faith. The Lord is showing up in your situation. He will restore your brokenness.

Today, I believe He wants to come in and breathe life over every area in your life where you've faced disappointment. He wants to heal those old wounds that are keeping you from seeing his goodness. Our Father is who He says He is. You can trust that He has good plans for you and that He will restore every broken area of your life. In His timing, He makes all things new. If you can continually shift your focus to Heaven, and refrain from constantly looking at how things appear in the natural, your joy will increase and you'll feel your strength begin to return.

Prayer: Heavenly Father, thank you for being with me in every area of my life. Thank you for never leaving my side. Forgive me for anytime that I have beheld my desires or beheld my problems, rather than beholding you. I ask that you would come and search my heart and uproot all areas of disappointment that have left me wounded. I believe that as you remove every wound of disappointment, I will arise and stand even taller in you. Thank you for repairing my brokenness. I love you Lord.

In Jesus name, amen.

Take Communion with the Lord.

Day 2

Taste and See

Lock eyes with the Lord.
Taste and see that HE is good.
Even in the midst of your pain and barrenness.
The one who created something out of nothing is there with you.

It's okay.
You're okay.
Taste and see...

Submit yourself to the Lord. He's drawing you closer.
The old wine's beginning to taste bitter...trade in the old wine for the new taste of Heaven.
Receive refreshing.
Relinquish the old.

Let the peace of God wash over you.
There's a NEW DAY coming to you where the pain of your past will be a distant memory.
YAHWEH has arrived.

Do you feel like you've been carrying around a bad taste in your mouth? When you think about believing and hoping for something again, does it make your stomach turn? If so, you're still carrying around the wine of last season! Trade in the old wine for the new taste of Heaven.

In the past you've tasted heartbreak, you've tasted betrayal, you've tasted shame...and right now, the Lord is wanting you to pour all of that out at His feet and receive the new wine. Allow the Lord to change your taste buds...to where you're no longer focused on savoring the taste of every hurt and disappointment but instead, you are forever and always savoring the taste of the Lord's goodness.

You can look back on every area where you've been hurt and disappointed and you can find God's goodness there. What did you learn during that season? How did you grow during that season? What wisdom did you gain? Even in your greatest moments of pain, the Lord is good and those moments have never been wasted. What the enemy tried to use to break you, the Lord was using to stretch you for His Kingdom purposes He's placed inside of you! He has been enlarging your capacity- creating a new wineskin for you to carry the new wine He's pouring into you.

Prayer: Heavenly Father, thank you for pouring your new wine over me. Thank you for refreshing me with the taste of your goodness. I give you everything from the past seasons I've walked that has put a bad taste in my mouth. I receive the taste of Heaven that you want to give me. Thank you for teaching me how to carry your new wine. Thank you for teaching me how to pour forth your new wine on those who are hurting so they can see your goodness and feel your love. I love you.

In Jesus name, amen.

Take Communion with the Lord.

Day 3

Undone By Your Love

Undo me in your love
and push my fear to the wayside.

Beckon me to fall into your arms and walk out your call.
One foot in front of the other.
I feel the trembling begin to cease...

I only feel peace.
Wrapped in your perfect peace.
I am undone in your love.

I **will** rise.
I will rise to the highest of mountains with you.

Through you.

In you.
Fortified in you.
An unstoppable force.
Defeating darkness and leading cohorts.
People of valor. Mighty in Stance.
Ready for war, while travailing in dance.
Pressed for purpose and made new by the pain.
Giving birth to greatness while whispering your name.
This whole time it's been unseen and my hands have been unable to touch...
But now it's being revealed...and it's all so much...
Your glory.

Your glory is pouring out like I've never seen before.
Everyone is in awe and my jaw has dropped to the floor.
I am undone by you.

I'm undone by your mighty ways.
I know now, I should've never questioned any of the pain.
You've known this entire time, exactly what you were birthing...
You told me to trust you,
despite all my hurting.

It was in the darkness, where this beauty has been formed.
And it was in the crushing, where I was lavishly adorned.
And it is in your presence, where I'm always finding new strength.

And every day...
I'm being made to look more like you.
And I can say...**it's worth it.**

I am undone by your love.

When we're faced with trial after trial, we can begin to feel undone. We start to feel like everything has unraveled in our life and it can feel chaotic and messy. But what if we looked at our mess as opportunities to be undone in God's love?

In our brokenness, the Lord comes close to us. He sees the chaos in our lives and the areas where everything has come "undone"...and He sits with us in that place. He pours His love out over us and moves us to feel. He causes us to feel what's been undone so we can give our tears, our worries, and our anxieties over to Him. He takes our chaos and brings order.

In the undoing, He undoes us in His love. Every day we're being formed to look more and more like Him. If I have to be undone, in order to look more like my Father...then bring on the undoing! Let's take these moments of brokenness and use them as moments to greater understand and grasp the depth of God's love for us.

And I pray that you, being rooted and established in love, may have power, together with all the Lord's holy people, to grasp how wide and long and high and deep is the love of Christ, and to know this love that surpasses knowledge—that you may be filled to the measure of all the fullness of God.

Ephesians 3:17-19

Prayer: Heavenly Father, thank you for undoing me in your love. Thank you for every moment I have faced that has caused me to feel like I'm unraveling. Because I know in those moments, I'm given opportunities to see the depth of your love for me. Thank you for rescuing me from the perspective that everything is falling or has fallen apart, and thank you for giving me a new perspective of being "undone in your love." Thank you for making me more and more like you every single day. I love you.
In Jesus name, amen.

Take Communion with the Lord.

Day 4

Like A Tree

My child, I am not withholding good things from you.
I know you've felt like you've sacrificed much with little in return.
I know it's felt like left and right you've had to watch the bridges burn.
But don't look so much towards the exterior to see what you have received.
Because what I've been doing in you...has been much like the growth of a tree.
Every time you've given me your yes, and you've told your flesh no...
Another root sprung up, down deep, and your roots have continued to grow...
Deep, deep, deep....into the ground is where you've been growing.

And in due time, all of your growth will begin showing.
I'm so proud of you and I've seen every sacrifice you've made.
I know it hasn't been easy but you've grown each time you've obeyed.
And even in the moments where it took some time for you to lay it all down,
I knew your heart would surrender and your faith would abound.
Surely, my warrior, surely you will see my goodness in the land of the living.
Look out into the distance, see those dry bones just sitting.
Open up your mouth and command those four winds to blow.
For everything that's been dead for so long, it's now time for their life to show!

For years the Lord has been teaching you, training you, and preparing you for the destiny that He has called you to. And for years, it has probably looked like you have nothing to show for everything that you've sowed! All the "yes's" you've given the Lord may have looked like they haven't yielded much fruit. But over the years, the Lord has been forging you into a strong oak tree. An oak tree of righteousness. It takes years for an oak tree to grow. And the growth of a tree, begins underneath. Without the growth of the roots, the tree wouldn't be able to stand firm. The Lord's been rooting you over all these years, to make you immovable and steadfast. And there comes a time where every seed you've sowed in the Lord will bear fruit. Continue yielding to the Lord's process because in due time, every seed that has looked dead and unfruitful in your life, will begin to reveal itself!

Prayer: Father, I pray that you would help me to see what you've done in my heart over these years. Allow me to see the areas in my life where you have grown me spiritually and emotionally. Forgive me Lord for any part of me that has wanted to rush ahead of you. Lord, I come under your submission and your timing. I trust that you know best and your ways are best. You know at what pace I need to grow and at what time you want to reveal a harvest. Thank you for being so patient with me. Increase my patience and my understanding Lord. I love you.

In Jesus name, amen.

Take Communion with the Lord.

Day 5

Glory, Glory, Glory

Glory, glory, glory.
Let it fall like rain.

Glory, glory, glory,
Come relieve this pain.

Glory, glory, glory,
Come sweeping in.

Glory, glory, glory,
Reach deep within.

Deep within the cave, I've been hidden for so long.
Longing to come out and to the world sing a new song.

Kneeling and weeping and desperate to see your face.
Seeking and searching, desiring to discover a trace...
A trace of your glory, I've been hoping to find.
But unexpectedly you've come, in a power so divine.
You've knocked me off my feet...out of the blue, you came!
For years I had been waiting... and proclaiming your name!
All of this time I'd been hidden, I was beginning to think...
My savior, my love...had forgotten about me...and each time my heart would sink.
But boy...was I wrong. I was so so wrong.
Now my head is bowed in humility as He shows himself strong.
The Lord has came to rescue me...and I'm in utter disbelief.
I'm trembling. I'm crying. And my knees feel weak.
But it's not like before.
These feelings aren't due to despair.
My mind has been blown...all this time He's been there!!!!
I'm filled with ecstatic joy and laughter begins to take over.
For a moment I felt ashamed for doubting the goodness of my Father...
But the Lord guides me quickly to let all of that go.
And He whispers deep within my heart to let joy explode.

Dance, my Warrior, Dance!
For the time is now...
To come out of the cave and be wonderfully wowed.
The magnitude of my glory will be like something you've never seen before.

And it's all because of your faithfulness to sit at my feet and endure.
Many trials you have walked and many days were filled with grief.
But your time of mourning, I'm sweeping under my feet.
Forget the old, It's gone, and I've done something new...
Take a look around...I've created all of this for you.
I'm placing much in your hands because you've been faithful with a little.
So go multiply, my warrior, and I'll swing my sickle!
I've chosen you for this work and that's why you've experienced all you did.
I purposely set you apart and intentionally kept you hid.
I did this to protect you and to draw you closer unto me.
I've taught you how to war, how to wait, and how to seek...
You're now ready for this ministry to be placed within your hands.
You won't come with merely impressive words...
this was all a part of my plan.
You're now filled with my power...and now everywhere you go...
Miracles, signs, and wonders will pour out of you in overflow.
I dwell in you, Warrior. And you, YOU, dwell in Me.
I trust you with my people...so now, its your time to lead.
Cast out the demons, heal the sick, and set the captives free.
Don't leave any stone unturned and remember you're doing this all through me.
My spirit empowers you for all the work you have ahead.
I've equipped you for this...to raise the sleepers from the dead.

My warrior, my love, my child...I've been anticipating this moment.
Every bit of substance I've poured into you is world changing and potent!
Great things you will do, and great things you will see, but the greatest of them all is your relationship with me.
Close your eyes for a moment, give thanks, and just breathe...
The adventure of your lifetime is finally in reach.
Lets run, lets laugh, lets cry, lets feel...
Feel my heart for the nations and my passion to heal.
Lets go, lets go, for the time is finally now!
Come out of hiding, my warrior, lets make our way through the crowd!
No obstacle can block you. No sight unseen.
The powers of darkness may try and stop you but you're a force in me.
The strength, endurance, and perseverance you carry...
Is all a result of the many years you've been buried.
It's time to put to use all the training you've received.
It's time to see the beauty that was created, that all started with a seed.
Open up your ears, do you hear the sound of their cries?
I'm now sending you out, to be my love, and my light.
Let's sing a new song,
together you and I.
Open up your mouth, and let the mystery arise.

Glory, glory, glory,
I'm drenched in your love.

Glory, glory, glory
You're more than enough.

Glory, glory, glory
There's nothing sweeter than you.

Glory, glory, glory,
My life has always been hidden in you.

What you thought was killing you over the past few years and sapping your strength, is actually what the Lord has been using to equip you for your calling. Everything that you've felt was sent to destroy you, was used as an instrument to deploy you!

The Lord has a place for you where He wants to use you greatly. He is sending you out to be a light to His people. You've experienced darkness, you've walked through hell, and you've seen God's hand pull you up and dust you off time and time again. Your faith has been stretched to where you know that anything, absolutely anything, is possible with God. You've been made ready to be a pure vessel for the Lord. All of your tears have been beautiful offerings to the Lord; of your life laid down. God's glory is going to shine through your life because you've submitted your life unto Him. Praise God today for every adverse situation you've faced, because it has crafted you into the person you are today- and there is a demographic of people who need your testimony.

They need to see Jesus in your life. And that's exactly what they're going to see. You've died to yourself, to come alive in Christ.

I have been crucified with Christ, and I no longer live, but Christ lives in me. The life I now live in the body, I live by faith in the Son of God, who loved me and gave himself for me.
Galatians 2:20

Prayer: Heavenly Father, you are so good. You are so beautiful. What a good Father, to know exactly what I need to grow stronger in you. Thank you for making me ready to serve your people well and with a pure heart. Thank you for emptying me of myself and filling me with your spirit and your love. Apart from you, I am nothing. And with you, I have everything. I love you.
In Jesus name, amen.

Take Communion with the Lord.

Day 6

Laying It Down

I'm laying down my weapons,
I can't seem to bear anymore.
I'm tired. I'm weak.
I don't think I can do this anymore.
My heart feels so heavy...
There's not much more of this that I can stand.
But in the midst of all my pain, I faintly hear you whispering...
that you have a greater plan.

But I'm hurting. I feel lost. And I'm not sure what else I can do.
I feel caged like a prisoner and I'm desperately needing rescue.
I'm trapped in the unknown, where there looks to be no light.
I've waged war it seems for years and I have nothing left to fight.

I'm lonely, vulnerable, and I'm weary from it all.
Lord, I know you hear me...please come rescue me...answer my call.

Lay down your weapons child and come lay down with me.
Your time of fighting is done for now, so leave the rest to me.
Let me remind you of the truth, that right now, you cannot see.
Although this battle has seemed ongoing, **you have the victory!**
I see the other side, and the light is closer than you know.
And although you feel weakest now, you're stronger than before.
Take this time to rest in me and let me fill you with new strength.
I'm so proud of you my warrior child, you've done better than you think.
Rest in me....just rest in me. Your deliverer and redeemer is here.
Your fragrance is so sweet to me, your presence is so dear.
Let me wrap you up in all my love and quiet all your fears.
Rest in me...just rest in me.
Your rescue is finally here.

Rest.

When you've been fighting for so long, sometimes fighting is all you know. You can find yourself relentlessly in battle mode-

waging war in the spirit and focusing your energy on getting free from your issues. But there are times that the Lord needs you to only *be still*. There are moments where the Lord needs you to know that this battle is His, and His alone. He knows your needs and He knows how to keep you safe. And in Him, you already have the victory anyway!

If you're weary from it all, it may be time for you to turn the fight mode off and just rest in your Father's arms knowing that He has you covered. You don't have to fight anymore. The Lord has gone before you and He's slaying your giants. Yield to His command to rest.

Moses answered the people, "Do not be afraid. Stand firm and you will see the deliverance the LORD will bring you today. The Egyptians you see today you will never see again. The LORD will fight for you; you need only to be still.
Exodus 14:13-14

Prayer: Heavenly Father, thank you for giving me the victory in all things! Praise you, God! Praise you for going before me and slaying every demonic force that tries to take me down. Thank you that I can lie down in green pastures with you, trusting you to lead me, and knowing you're fighting for me.
In Jesus name, amen.

Take Communion with the Lord.

Day 7

Warrior Child

Oh weary one, cling on to me.
Everything you need is found in my presence.

Oh weary one, sing songs to me.
Your praise is one of your greatest weapons.

Oh weary one, a new day is here
and I'm filling you up with new strength.

Oh weary one, it's your time to fly.
You're going to go to great lengths.

Take my hand and let me show you around.
Let me unveil the mysteries...the greatest that could be found.
My Kingdom is yours and I delight to give it to you.

Come linger a little longer...I love being here with you.
Cast down every worry and every care at my feet.
Express your heart and your soul and tell me where you feel weak.
Although I already know the inner truths of your heart...
I long to hear you open up, and intimately tell me every part.
Silence the voice of the enemy,
he has no right to your mind.
Capture every thought that tries to exalt itself above your divine.
Step into your authority, it's time for you to speak up!
Use the voice I've given you, tell the enemy "enough is enough!"
You are a warrior my child, no longer identify as weary.
You're coming out of that place, it's time to start seeing clearly.
Take my hand and let me remind you of who are...
You are a royal priesthood and you're destined to go far.
You have a voice to shake the nations and darkness trembles at your light.
You're anointed to set the captives free and chosen to set things right.
You'll bring justice to this world and you'll proclaim the words I speak.
You'll be fearless in following my command and will impart boldness to the weak!
My warrior child, you'll be absolutely unstoppable in everything that you do.

So take heart and remain steadfast, because you live in me and
I live in YOU!

Oh warrior child, it's time to rise up.
You're set time to lead is now.

Oh warrior child, I've prepared you for this...
Cease your mind from wondering how.

Oh warrior child, I've waited for this.
Your moment to be sent out has arrived.

Oh warrior child, you were created for this
Walk out your calling, its time to thrive!

It's time to take a look in the mirror and speak to the core of who you are. Yes, I know you've felt weary. I know this weariness has affected every area of your life. It's probably affected your confidence and has attempted to poison the view you have of yourself. It has probably left you questioning many past decisions in your life and maybe you've even questioned if you've been hearing from the Lord all this time or if you've been hearing incorrectly.

It's time to step out of the identity of "weary." This weariness has hung around for far too long and it's attempted to infiltrate your identity. But that ends today! Today, you are going to affirm yourself in Christ and speak to your identity: **you are a warrior for Christ!** You are not weary and defeated, you are a warrior and victorious! Shame has got to go. Depression has got to go. Anxiety has got to go. Every bit of weariness must leave in Jesus name.

The Lord is setting you free today from the snare of no longer feeling capable. He is setting you free from the lies you've believed that things will never change. You have an eternal reward waiting on you- and things will change!!! You still have work for the Kingdom and the Lord has GOOD plans in store for you. Release your weariness to the Lord. **He is cloaking you in new strength today. Receive it by faith.**

Prayer: Heavenly Father, thank you for cloaking me in new strength. Thank you for making me mighty and strong in you. I receive the refreshing you're giving me today. I trust in your goodness to heal every aching part of my heart and to bind up my broken wings! I believe that in you, I will fly again! I am mounting up with wings like an eagle and it's all because of your faithfulness to empower me and fill me with new strength! Praise you Lord! In Jesus name, amen.

Take Communion with the Lord.

Day 8

You Knew

You led me here.
All along you led me here.

It was written in your book of life.
You knew every storm I'd face.
Every moment I'd feel forgotten.
Every time my head would fall in defeat.
You knew every tear I'd shed.
Every moment I'd feel rejected.
And every moment I'd feel terribly weak.
You knew.

But you chose that path.
The path for me that looked unlike anything I would've chosen for myself.

You knew.

You knew what I needed.
You knew the tension necessary to birth what you had placed deep inside.
You knew how to call me into the deep so I'd turn towards you and hide.
Hidden under the shelter of your wings, you knew just how to point me in that direction.
You knew how to place me in the darkest valleys and how to teach me you're my protection.
You knew how to shape me through trials and tribulation and what experiences you needed me to walk through.
You knew what would change my ways of thinking and what would make my heart brand new.
You knew.
So thank you father.
For every bit of suffering you planned for me to endure.
For every tear I had to cry and every day I had to question "how much longer"
Thank you for producing in me something that far outweighs every day I've ever suffered.
This glory revealed in me has been worth it...
And I just want to say thank you.
Thank you that...
You knew.

Everything you've walked through throughout your life, has

been sent by the master potter to mold you! It's all been a set up from the Lord. The Lord is very meticulous and intentional in all that He does! If you were the one to craft your life and decide what happens to you, I'm quite certain you probably wouldn't add hardships and chaos into your timeline. But if that were the case, and you chose to live an easy-going life with no uphill battles, how many opportunities would you have for growth? How many opportunities would you have to see God's mighty hand move mountains for you? How many people would you be able to help if you've never gone through trials and tribulations?

Those experiences that have currently brought you to a place of deep weariness, the Lord is actually going to use to thrust you forward. Because you've walked through many trials, you've grown so much closer to Christ! You have gained so much knowledge and wisdom. And you now know exactly what other people need to hear who are currently in the same positions that you've been in. Your testimony will bring life to others! So thank God! All this time, He knew. He knew how those fires would refine you! He knew how the crushing would produce oil in you! He knew!

Prayer: Heavenly Father, thank you for crushing me to produce beautiful oil for you. Thank you for knowing exactly what I need to experience to be able to walk out the call that you've planned for me! I am so glad that you are Lord over my life and you are the one to cause things to happen! I thank you for protecting me throughout this journey of life! I thank you for wrapping your loving arms around me and helping me to stand up after falling over and over again. I love you.

In Jesus name, amen.

Take Communion with the Lord.

Day 9

The Space Between

In the space between I find myself warring...
Warring between my past and the future I cannot yet see.
To choose comfort now, would leave me missing out on many grandeur things you've spoken over me.
At arms reach, I can grab ahold of what's in front of me...
It seems to taste good...but deep within my spirit, I sense this isn't what you've promised me.
But it's here now, and I'm so weary...I'm so tired of waiting.
I'm thirsty. And every inch of my being is craving...
Craving change.

In the space between...nothing is different.
I've been holding onto the words you spoke: "new beginnings."
And I have yet to see, this place you've spoken over me.

But I'm holding on...because I know you're a good father.
And now I'm letting go...of what is so easily attainable now, in this moment.
I don't want the counterfeit, Lord. I want the real thing.
And even though I'm in the space between, I desire to trust you deeper with everything.
So hold me tighter Lord than you've ever held me before.
I'm letting go of my past once again and I desperately need help to firmly close the door.

In the space between...I'm trusting you with everything that feels so uncertain.
I'm completely in the dark, and I'm waiting for you to pull back the curtain.
I trust deep within my heart, that you have so much you want to give me.
And I believe change is around the corner, and soon I'll finally be able to see...
All of the good things that you have prepared, all specifically, just for me!
Every "good" thing I let go of, I believe that you're giving me greater.
Turning ashes into beauty, what a wonderful creator!
So I'm leaning on you in this moment of heart wrenching affliction
and I'm letting go of my old thoughts and I'm beholding your depiction.

In the space between, you say this is good for me.

I'm dying to my flesh and I'm learning to trust you in the unseen.
I'm learning to discern what you have for me versus what you do not.
And I'm being rid of all selfishness and being reminded of your grace which was bought.
What a hefty price you paid for me, to bring me into your presence.
Why would I want to forsake that for just a slight moment of pleasure?
When deep down in my spirit, I know that I have the greatest pleasure around.
And it's here....in the space between, that my true treasure... has been found.

There is the "good thing" and then there is the "God thing." The "God thing" often requires patience. There's a process typically tied to what the Lord wants to bestow upon you. He is such a good Father that he wants to prepare you to be able to carry the magnitude of what He wants to place in your hands. The "God thing" requires a preparation that will allow you to steward the "God thing" well.

The "good thing"...is usually readily attainable. It looks good and it brings immediate gratification. It will often check off many desires from your list, not all of them, but in your mind it will be "good enough". It brings immediate joy. There's no waiting or preparing...it's just available! But...the kicker is, it's not sustainable.

Although it can be attained quickly, it can also be lost quickly. The joy you initially felt in the beginning will also leave quickly! Not to mention, chaos is also tied to the "good thing" because it's not the will of God!

It's important to be close to the Fathers' feet because discernment is needed when it comes to the "good thing" and the "God thing!" The "good thing" is incredibly deceptive. If you're not careful, you can miss the subtle warning signs that this isn't what the Lord has for you.

I know how tiring it is to wait for what God has for you. But let's ponder this question for a moment...what's your hearts greatest, number one, desire? If our number one desire is to intimately know the one who formed us and knew us before we were born, we can never be disappointed. All of the pleasure and joy we're seeking from these temporary things can be found in the Father's presence. He is the greatest treasure there is. Make Him the object of your affection. Everything else will fade away. The wait becomes harder when we behold our temporary desires over our Creator. Behold Him, and you will feel your strength begin to return. He has everything you need and He IS everything you need.

Prayer: Heavenly Father, I ask that you would give me wisdom and discernment concerning what is from you and what is not from you. Help me to be patient in all things and behold you above all things. Forgive me for anytime that my heart has been set and focused on what I want, opposed to being set and focused on you. Close any doors in my life that are not from you. If I'm currently holding onto "good things" that aren't from you, I pray that you would remove those things from my life and give me strength to not

return to them. Give me strength to endure in the waiting. Help me to remember that it's such a blessing that you have been preparing me for your gifts so that I don't receive them immaturely and squander them. Thank you Lord.
In Jesus name, amen.

Take Communion with the Lord.

Day 10

Open Eyes

My eyes are closed.
I'm trusting in you. Although, I cannot see a thing.
Lead me into green pastures in which you have promised me.
I lay down before you and I submit my life to you.
Under your submission, I'm given the command to rest.
I'm resting in your presence, being filled with your sweet aroma.
There's nothing like the fragrance of the Lord.
It awakens my senses.
You're bringing me to life again.
That which was once dead...is coming to life again.

My eyes are closed.
But I'm sensing change in the air.
I feel your wind blowing around me.

I feel all that was dead, is being raised to its feet.
Redemption...recompense...repair.
I feel you repairing what has been broken.
I feel resurrection power swirling around me.
You didn't bring me to this space to have me surrounded by death.
You brought me here to be surrounded by victory.
I hear you singing a new song over me...
A song of victory.
A song of "look at what I've done!"
"Look at what I've done for my laid down lover!"

I'm pleased to be your laid down lover.
I'm in awe of how you've turned this wasteland into an abundant garden.
Life is all around me.
And I'm singing a new song with you.

My eyes are open.
My eyes are open to see the goodness of the Lord in the land of the living.

There is a sweet sound to what the Lord is doing in your life right now. It's the sound of restoration. The Lord is singing over you. He loves you and He delights in you. He wants the best for you because you're His child. I know it feels dark and nothing may make sense right now...but the Lord just needs you to trust Him and rest in Him. He's working out things for you that you can't even see. But soon you will.

There are other moving pieces connected to you that the Lord is bringing into order. He is making ways where there seems to be no way. He is putting the pieces together for you- He is moving with intention and precision. You can trust that the Lord is the master connecter. You will look up and see the goodness of the Lord in the land of the living. You will see how He brought it all together. You will be in awe with how the Lord performs in your life.

The LORD your God is with you, the Mighty Warrior who saves. He will take great delight in you; in his love he will no longer rebuke you, but will rejoice over you with singing."
Zephaniah 3:17

Prayer: Heavenly Father, thank you for being the master connecter. Thank you for being the restorer of all things. I trust that you are doing things right now that I have no idea of. I trust that you have my best interest in mind. You know what I need. Help me to rest in you and cease from my worrying. I want what you have for me. I don't want to grow weary, throw in the towel, and settle...I want to thrive in you and receive your best. Cover me and help me to see your goodness even in my weariness. I love you Lord.
In Jesus name, amen.

Take Communion with the Lord.

Day 11

I'm Right Here

I want to be where you are.
Take me into your loving arms.
The distance between us feels unbearable.
I need to feel your touch.
Oh, how I wish I could feel your hug.
What a hug that would be from my wonderful Savior!
Oh, how I know I would just melt.
Just one touch of your hand would instantaneously make it all better.
Please make it all better...

Child, I'm right here.
I promise I'm right here with you.
There's nothing that separates you from I.
Close your eyes, get quiet, and sit still in my presence.

Do you see me reaching out my arms?
Lean into me and melt into my presence.
Melt right here, in me.
Allow me to melt away every worry, every fear, and wipe away every tear that has been falling from your face.
Allow me to bring you into the fullness of my joy today.
Allow me to bring you into the fullness of my joy everyday.
The portion I give you is sweet and it is enough.
Just sit with me. Wait on me. Trust in me.
Reach out your hands and allow me to pour my healing oil over you.
Receive.
Receive what I'm doing right now.
I'm washing it all away right now.
Just lean on me.
And know that I'm right here.

He's available. He's always available. When you're in need of deep comfort, the Lord is our reservoir that never runs dry. In those moments where it feels like you are alone and you feel sick to your stomach due to grief, the Lord is in the midst waiting for you to pour out all your concerns to Him. He's waiting for your tears to soak the hem of His garment as a beautiful sacrifice unto Him. He will stay close to you and will hold your hand through it all. **You're not alone.** Even though you feel alone and feel like no one understands, God sees you. He won't allow you to stay in this place of deep sadness forever. His nature is to redeem. The Lord is your portion, so put your hope in Him. Other people may have left you, but your Heavenly Father never will. He is faithful to be by your side with all the love and affection your soul could ever need. Sit at his feet and receive His healing today.

Prayer: Heavenly Father, thank you that I can trust you to never forsake me. I receive the healing that you want to pour out on me today. You've seen how weary I've grown. Strengthen me with your love. Empower me to feel alive again. Remove this heaviness from my chest. Fill the emptiness in my body. Overcome me with your love and comfort. Make it so tangible that I can't help but to weep because I'm overwhelmed by your love. Help me to feel your warm embrace. I love you Lord and I need you. I need you more and more every day. Thank you for being right by my side.
In Jesus name, amen.

Take Communion with the Lord.

Day 12

The Deliverer is Here

I'm heartsick for change.
I've been beaten down by my circumstances.
Many days it feels like I'm fighting an uphill battle.
I take a few steps forward and it seems I go ten steps backwards.

Where is my deliverer?
Oh, where is my deliverer?

Do you hear my heart cries, do you see my hearts defeat?
Do you see how day and night, I lay everything at your feet?
Do you see my barrenness?
Do you see the dry, dry land?
Do you see how in every circumstance, I reach out to hold your hand?

Do you hear me calling out for you...
crying out for your salvation...
to pull me up from this slippery rock and place me on your firm foundation?

Where is my deliverer?
Oh, where is my deliverer?

Day and night I've seen you, my child.
I've seen every single tear that's fell from your face.
I've heard your persistent prayers and I'm meeting you in this place.
I'm coming down from Heaven to visit you with my touch.
I'm making everything new, *the time is now,* you've seen enough!
Your time of grieving is done and it's time for you to experience laughter and cheer!
So, lift up your head Warrior, because your Deliverer is here!

Take heart! Your Savior has come! He has come to be the lifter of your soul and the lifter of your head. His wind is blowing on you, drying every tear and rejuvenating you, so you can move in a fresh wind!

Look all around you. What you see now, will not be what you see when the Lord breaks through for you. He is breaking open the way for you! Your tears of sadness will turn to tears of joy. No longer will you be crying out in desperation, but instead you'll be crying out in celebration! The Lord is perfecting what concerns you!

Prayer: Heavenly Father, I trust that you're delivering me! I trust that you're saving me from all that has beaten me down. Thank you for encouraging my spirit with your truth and reminding me of how much you care for me. You're the sweetest Father. Forgive me for any moments where I've doubted if you'd come through for me. Forgive me for moments where I've been angry with you. I love you Lord.
In Jesus name, amen.

Take Communion with the Lord.

Day 13

Pleasure

How can I find pleasure in pain?
Worldly pleasure is in arms reach but my spirit will not have it.
You say you're the ultimate pleasure, and I believe it, but right now...I only feel pain.
If I choose the world, I'd be abandoning you.
And although this pleasure is available now, I know there's nothing more painful than being without you.
Being apart from you, I could not stand.
But tell me...
How can I find pleasure in pain?

A pool of pleasure is available to you.
But you must be willing to sit at my feet and linger.
Linger until you feel pleasure.
I am not a God who loves to watch you cry.

I do not find joy in watching you suffer.
What I do find joy in, is knowing what's being produced inside of you.
I do find joy in knowing that I have everything you need.
And I also find joy in you discovering and feeling my pleasure.
It's there. Even in the pain, it is there.
I know you are hurting and I know this doesn't feel good.
I know you'd love to have a taste of what's in front of you right now.
But I'm asking you to trust me...and to taste me.
Taste my goodness in the middle of your suffering.
What I offer you, is far greater than anything this world can offer you.
My ways are higher....my thoughts are higher...my plans are higher...
Whatever you think is good, I have better in store for you.
Sit in this pool with me and just linger.
Let the pain of yesterday and the pain of today get made clean in the waters of my love.
Let my love wash over you.
It's enough. It's more than enough.
In fact, it's overwhelming.
If you sit and linger here for a while, you'll be overcome by the pleasure my presence brings.
It's better than anything you've ever tasted.

Let's dig new wells together.
New wells of my glory.
They're located deep within you.

They're places where I'll pour my spirit out and fill every
longing and every void...
where the things of this world will grow strangely dim
and the only thing you will desire is the taste of my presence!

There is a better way that is calling out to you! The way of the Lord! The way of the Lord will not leave you thirsting for more unlike the things of this world. When we've experienced years of longings unfulfilled and we've grown tired of it all, we can at times find ourselves vulnerable to slipping up and attempting to create pleasure for ourselves that isn't going to last. The only lasting pleasure there is, is the pleasure that's discovered at the Lord's feet. The longer you sit in His presence, the more you will be filled with His comfort and pleasure. So, linger a little longer. You never know what your Father may have for you if you just wait on Him.

Prayer: Lord, forgive me for anytime I've attempted to seek worldly pleasure. Help me to sit with you longer and be filled with your comfort and peace. Provide pleasure in this place of pain for me. Give me eyes to see, ears to hear, and a heart to feel, the pleasure you want to bring to me today. I love you so much!
In Jesus name, amen.

Take Communion with the Lord.

Day 14

From Captivity to Captivation

Captivate me with your presence
as I feel prisoner to my circumstances.
No where to go, no where to turn.
I'm helpless.
But you, you're not.
You're my answer.
You're my rescuer.
You're my redeemer.
I'm calling on your name.
Save me.

If I have to sit in this pain any longer, then captivate me with your love...
so that this pain I'm feeling disintegrates and I'm only left sitting in a pool of your love.

I need you to wrap me up in your wings of refuge and take me
to the highest of mountains with you.
Take the sting of this pain away with your healing Balm of
Gilead.
Turn this heart sick land into a land that is well and thriving!
A land that is flourishing...where life bursts forth!
Take me in as your prisoner of love.
Make my pain a distant memory and turn my mourning into
dancing.
Let me dance these shackles off...
Let me celebrate you, the God I serve.

I may be in captivity.
I may feel imprisoned.
But I know you're a safe chamber for me to place my hope in.
Help my heart to bubble up with joy in the pure truth that
you are worthy of celebration!
You are worthy of it all.
I will dance these shackles off in the chamber of your love.

Those moments of being at the end of yourself and completely helpless are the greatest opportunities for God to reveal Himself to you as the Great Redeemer and Restorer. You may feel like there is no way out of the situation you're in. It may feel like rescue will never come. But the Lord has promised to rescue you. Take your eyes off of your problems today and place your eyes on your Father. He is your rescuer and His love will break any and every chain that has attached itself to you. In Him, you have freedom.

You may feel all alone and stuck in a stagnant place, but that is not your end!!! Change your mindset today. You aren't in captivity or imprisoned by your circumstances...you are entrusted in the hands of God, protected from evil, and blessed to be captivated by His presence.

Prayer: Heavenly Father, thank you for captivating me with your presence. Thank you for catching my attention and revealing more of your character to me. Thank you for changing my outlook and helping me to see that in you, I am never stuck. I love you Lord! In Jesus name, amen.

Take Communion with the Lord.

Day 15

Certain

I am certain that I'll see the goodness of the Lord in the land
of the living.
Even though I have days where I feel impatient, and days
where all I do is cry...
I believe in the goodness of my Father to rescue me and to give
me a brand new life!
Although I'm so tired and my knees are feeling so weak...
I'm going to lift my arms to praise Him and stand strong
upon my feet
I'm going to take the strength I have, and march forward
towards the new land.
Even though I don't know where I'm going, I'm trusting He
will lead me with His hand.

This journey has been long but I feel in my heart that we must be so much closer!
Any day now things could change so I'll remain hopeful and continue rejoicing!
My hearts been really heavy so there are days I struggle to remain in joy.
But I hear my Father's voice reminding me to lift up a praise and celebrate with great noise.
I feel His presence commanding me to silence my thoughts and to simply behold Him.
To set my gaze on His face, give thanks, and yield to the molding.
I'm clay in His hands...and I can find comfort in what He's shaping.
Even though it's been painful...I can trust in what He's making.

The Lord knows what He is doing! We could never understand the intricacies of His thoughts or plans. And that's why it can be so easy for us to feel uncertain in circumstances that may look or feel chaotic. Refinement of the Lord is never comfortable and it usually comes packaged in a process that seems daunting and feels never-ending. The processing and molding of the Lord doesn't usually feel good! It requires change, self-denial, humbling, and often times great loss is experienced. It goes against our human nature.

But in Christ, we're dying daily to our flesh. Death doesn't feel good but it makes room for new life to be birthed!

Think about Job. Imagine how much his faith grew and his character expanded after walking through the seasons He did, suffering great loss, yet remaining faithful in his beliefs, and then he was able to see the Lord not only restore his fortunes, but double them!

God is using the momentary afflictions of your life to prepare you for eternity! He's refining you through these troubles to make you a pure bride. You will see His goodness! Keep holding on and do not lose faith! The Lord is working ALL things together for your good.

We know that all things work together for the good of those who love God, who are called according to his purpose.
Romans 8:28

Prayer: Heavenly Father, thank you for looking out for me! Even though this walk has been excruciatingly painful, I know that what you are producing in me is far greater than this pain I've been experiencing. Thank you for readying me to be a pure bride for your return! I love you Lord and I am so glad that I am your chosen child. Thank you that you keep your eyes on me and you're mindful of me! Thank you for your loving discipline. You're such a good Father!
In Jesus name, amen.

Take Communion with the Lord.

Day 16

Tell Them

Child,
Do you not see this wide open space I've placed you in?

Your eyes see barrenness.
My eyes see opportunity.

Your heart screams danger.
My heart whispers safe place.

In the place of the unknown, I make myself more known.
Isn't me that you want to see?
Didn't you ask to encounter me in a new way?
You've never seen me in this way before...and I want to show you a new side of me.

But the only way I can, is by taking you through this barren land and leading you around everything that once was.
Everything that you once held tightly, I allowed to slip through your fingers.
I allowed you to encounter death after death after death.
So you can encounter glory to glory to glory.
Watch what I do in this new land I've brought you to!
What has been empty will become inhabited.
What produced nothing, will begin to produce an abundance.
What once was dry, will become a well watered garden.
I didn't leave you here to thirst.
But I brought you here to thirst for my righteousness.
And now that you're seeing more clearly and you've been emptied more of yourself,
I'm ready to downpour my glory and my goodness on your land.
Yes child, you will see my goodness in the land of the living and it will be put on display for the world to see.
They saw you walk in shame, now they will see you shine in my name.

The family I'm bringing you, the ministry I'm bringing you, the wealth I'm bringing you...
It's a sign.
It's a wonder.
It's a message to my people of what happens when you choose to leave Egypt and yield to the suffering in the wilderness.
It's what happens when you choose me over and over again rather than choosing the world.

It's what happens when you let go of your life and you choose to bear my cross.
You will not suffer in shame any longer.
A double portion I'm pouring out over you.
Now, open up your mouth wide so I can fill it.
Speak to my people and tell them what you experienced and how I came through for you.
Tell them about the countless tears you cried and the weariness you felt.
Tell them how you never stopped believing in me and my goodness.
Tell them about the people who left you and the people I called you to leave.
Tell them about my faithfulness as your Father to never leave you or forsake you.
Tell them how I made myself known to you and how I would whisper in your ear when you had no strength to continue on.
Tell them how I took your barren land and turned it into a thriving land for the world to see.
Tell them that if they yield and surrender to me, they will get to taste my suffering and taste my glory.
Tell them that the taste of me far outweighs anything their lips could ever touch in this world.
I need you to open your mouth and tell them.
Do not hold back.
You've been barren for some time, but now you're giving birth to everything at once!
And as you birth out these promises I've made you, I need you to **profess to the world of my goodness!**

Don't allow shame to keep you from speaking up.
For such a time as this, I'm raising you up and I'm raising you out of everything that "once was."
Enter the new, my child.
Enter the new.

The Lord has been constructing a mighty testimony in your life! It's a testimony that others will hear and they'll be unable to deny that God is who He says He is. You've faced many storms and I'm sure you've also faced great loss. And in the midst of all your pain, I'm sure there has been much questioning! But God! God has had a purpose for you this entire time. Even when it looked like total death, the Lord has always had resurrection in His mind.

There are blessings the Lord has been waiting to release to you at the perfect timing. You may have suffered great loss but you have great reward in store for you. Many situations you've walked through may have caused you great shame. But let go of that shame! Shame will keep you from speaking up and God needs your voice! He needs you to open up and share what He has done in your life! When you see breakthrough in your life and you experience healing, be ready to tell others what God has done for you! Your testimony can and will save others!

Prayer: Heavenly Father, I pray that you would remove any shame that I've been carrying around lately. Lord, I thank you for the restoration that you have planned for me. I thank you for using the storms in my life to make me more like you and for teaching me

to trust you deeper. God, I pray that you would anoint my mouth to speak and give me the boldness to open up and share what you have done for me! Help me to not hold back and to be overflowing with gratitude for all that you've done for me! I love you Lord.
In Jesus name, amen.

Take Communion with the Lord.

Day 17

Take Another Step

Could you light up the path Father?
Child, just trust me and take another step.
But I can't see where I am going. What if I stumble?
Child, just trust me and take another step.
But what if I get attacked and get stuck where I'm at?
Child, just trust me and take another step.
Take another step my child…into the darkness.
Oh, you of little faith…let your faith RISE UP.
Would I lead you as far as I already have, then turn around and leave you?
Do you not know my character?

I need you to trust me and take another step.
Remember how I made ways out of no ways for you.

Remember when you took that step of faith and you got to see miracles in front of you.
Remember all the times I carried you through the darkness and soon you were able to see where I was taking you.

Oh yes, Father. Forgive me Father.
I believe in you Father, but help my unbelief.
This time it just feels darker and the path feels longer...even though I don't even know where we're going.
But I'm going to trust you. And I'm going to take another step....

The longer you walk with Christ and take the steps of faith He has asked you to, the more radical those steps of faith will become. The steps of faith required for your new season, will always be greater than last season! This is because God wants to stretch you! As he stretches you, the more your trust for Him grows and the more you're able to see Him move mightily in your life. God desires to take you from glory to glory in Him, but in that, He needs to take you from faith to greater faith.

The Lord may be asking you to do something right now that requires you to trust Him at a greater level of faith. It may be very difficult and quite scary, but you must remind yourself how He has always come through for you in the past. The Lord is with you wherever you go. I promise you, if He's asking you to take another step forward, He will be right there with you. If you mess up, He will correct you. You cannot go wrong when you're in your Father's hands and you're seeking to do His will. To be obedient to the Lord's promptings is the absolute best thing you can do! He isn't going to lead you to a place and then suddenly abandon you. He has a way for you and all you need to do is just take one step forward! He will lead you in the dark. One step at a time.

Prayer: Dear Lord, thank you for your presence. Thank you that your presence leads me and shows me where to go. Thank you that in the dark, I can trust you. Thank you that in the dark, I don't need to see. I only need to hold your hand and take one step at a time. Thank you for removing any anxiety or worry from my heart. I know you're a good Father and you would never lead me astray. Thank you for your direction and guiding me with so much love. I know you won't let me fall. Thank you for teaching me to trust you more and more. Please forgive me God for any time that I have not trusted you fully. All I want to do is to trust and obey you. Help me to grow in you and be quick to listen. I don't want to delay my actions to your instructions. I want to follow you even when it's terrifying. Thank you for giving me boldness and courage to walk out the plans you have for me. One step at a time. Thank you for quieting my mind and my fears. I love you Lord.

In Jesus name, amen.

Take Communion with the Lord.

Day 18

Could It Really Be?

Could it really be?
Could it really be that you are leaving your throne to visit earth and set things straight?
What is man that you are so mindful of him?
How could we be so lucky to have a Father like you who goes to war for his children?
I feel you leaning towards me reminding me that I am only to rest right now and to allow you to handle the rest.
You're putting my enemies to shame.
You're closing the mouths of the wicked who have spoken evil towards your children and you're bringing a measure of justice and recompense that the world has yet to ever see.

What a good Father. What a good judge. What a lover.

You love justice.
I cant imagine the anticipation you've been feeling to make things right.
I believe deep in my heart that it's that time. It's the time where you're going to act.
You've heard our cries. You've seen our faithfulness to steward your presence and undergo the crushing.
We've poured out an offering of praise on your altar.
The ceremony of celebrating the victory you're bringing us.
Of celebrating the God we serve.
The ceremony before the ceremony.
You're bringing us together to rise up and take back what's yours.
Together, a fortified army, after resting...you're sending us out to be a light to the nations.
What ease we will be able to flow in knowing that our Father has rescued us so we can go and rescue others.
Thank you for coming Lord.
Thank you for stepping down from heaven and setting things straight.
We will faithfully carry the torches you have handed us and give honor where honor is due.
Praise be to God. Our mighty God who goes to war for us and brings his children the victory every time.

The Lord is righting every wrong. As you feel things shaking, know that God is making all things right! The Lord has been waiting for the perfect time to release His justice in your life.

The Lord does not standby without acting. Where injustice has occurred, you can expect the Lord to act. Just because you haven't seen justice yet, doesn't mean it's not coming. It is.

Heavenly Father, thank you for acting in my life. Thank you for showing up and bringing justice. I know you won't leave me forsaken. You deserve all the glory, praise, and honor. Thank you Lord, thank you.
In Jesus name, amen.

Take Communion with the Lord.

Day 19

Count Your Blessings

Count your many blessings.
Count them one by one.
My work has been finished, your freedom already won.
Walk with your head lifted high, warrior child. You always have the victory.
Your faithfulness to abide in me will forever be my favorite symphony.
New songs, lets sing together, about the battles we have won.
I've placed my spirit in you, you are one with the Father and the Son.
Whatever tries to ail you or steal from your strength...
Give it a taste of your tenacity, showing you'll endure to great lengths.
Any pressure that builds upon you, remember, it will always forge you stronger.

It's increasing your capacity and teaching you how to run your race longer.
What looks like it will defeat you, will actually be pulverized to dust.
Because I'm the one fighting through you, so in me, place your trust!

It doesn't matter how insurmountable the obstacle may appear, your God is bigger. Yahweh will conquer every giant that attempts to kill, steal, and destroy your life. If you've been going around and around the same mountain, facing the same giants over and over again, it can sometimes feel like you're fighting a losing battle. But the truth of the matter is, there's an appointed time of freedom that the Lord has set for you. You will not have to fight relentlessly forever. Begin speaking life over your battles today. You are victorious in every battle that comes your way because it is your Lord, God who is fighting for you! He will put your enemies to shame!

Prayer: Heavenly Father, thank you that you go before me and you fight for me. Thank you for demolishing every giant that has stood in my path for entirely too long. I can do none of this apart from you. I need you in every aspect of my life. Change my mindset Lord. Never allow me to look at a battle and feel defeated. Help me to always remember that no matter what battle I face, I have the victory! I have the victory only because you are the one to fight for me! Thank you for the strength you're giving me to endure every trial and tribulation that comes my way. You are so faithful Father. I love you Lord.

In Jesus name, amen.

Take Communion with the Lord.

Day 20

Lion Heart

Where are my lionhearts?
The ones who will fiercely preach my name?
The ones who are not worried about rocking the boat?
They're not worried about people pleasing and they have no desire to tickle ears.

My lionhearts...
Those that are brave and courageous and they're ready to set out wherever I tell them to go.
They have willingly laid their life down and counted the cost...and they know that I am worth it.

Where are my lionhearts?
They are filled with a fire but they are also oozing with my love.

It's their love that bubbles up such a deep passion within
them for justice in the world.
They're passionate about setting the captives free and releasing
prisoners from their chains.
They have compassion for the underdogs. They have compassion for the weak. They have compassion for the vulnerable.
They have compassion for the misfits.

My lionhearts...
They only do what they see me doing.
They only speak what they hear me saying.
Where are my lionhearts?

I'm calling you to the forefront my lionhearts.
I'm calling you to pioneer a new movement.
I'm commissioning you to rise from your weariness and I'm
clothing you in new strength.
GO Lionheart, GO!
The time is now for you to GO!
Roar.
Lion of mine, roar.
The time is now for you to, ROAR.

You can't and won't be hidden forever! The Lord needs you! He needs your roar! He needs your boldness! He needs your passion! The world needs you to rise up and take the position the Lord has given you to spread His love and His truth everywhere you go. You were made for this. You were created by God and for God.

He's prepared you to run and go forth in the power of His name. You weren't created to be a silent bystander whose afraid to rock the boat! You were created to create movement in God's name.

People ridiculed Jesus and many didn't understand the way He moved and the way He spoke. He was hated by many because they didn't understand who He was. When you rise up to go forth boldly in your calling, there will be many who don't understand you. Many who ridicule you and are offended by you. Go forth anyways. Speak anyways. Share the love of God anyways. You are a Lion in Christ. You are meant to ROAR.

Prayer: Heavenly Father, armor me with boldness and courage. May I make you proud in the way that I passionately share the gospel, completely unashamed! May I be bold as a Lion in all that I do for your kingdom. If there is any desire to people please hiding within me, I ask that you would remove it. Help me to only care about pleasing you and only you. Help me to speak up when you tell me to! To speak your truth in love. Make me a force to be reckoned with. Help me to lead others to you! Give me the words to speak and help me to have the faith to just open up my mouth and allow you to flow out as you please. I love you Lord.
In Jesus name, amen.

Take Communion with the Lord.

Day 21

Too Far to Turn Back Now

You've come too far to turn back now.
Wait with me.
Your deliverance is scheduled and it's coming right on time.
I'm not withholding any good thing from you.
I know what you need and I know when you need it.
Silence your soul and find peace in my presence.
I'm writing your story and everything is going as planned.

Your suffering is for purpose.
Your waiting is for purpose.
Your pain is for purpose.

If this feels heavy, you're carrying more than you're supposed to.
My yoke is easy and my burden is light.

Sit with me and pour out your heart.
Tell me how you feel.
Express your anger and your sadness.
Tell me how you don't understand but you're choosing to trust me anyways.
Release the load you've been carrying.
Hand every worry and every anxiety over to me.
Once you express your heart and put your circumstances in my hands,
I can flow my rivers of peace over every inch of your being.
I care for you.
Don't be scared to share your heart with me.
We have relationship, and what good is a relationship if we're not communicating our feelings.
Seek me and know me and you will find me.

You will find me in your suffering.
You will find me in your waiting.
You will find me in your pain.

I'm here...
Right here.
You've come too far to turn back now.

God wants all of your heart today and everyday! He doesn't shy away from your anger. In fact, he understands all of your emotions! It's okay to feel all of the feelings you've been feeling due to the pain of your waiting and the grief you've experienced while enduring tough circumstances. You are not a robot. God created us to feel. But He's also given us a way to release. There's a time for everything...there is a time for feeling your emotions with the Lord and there's a time of releasing your emotions to the Lord. Open up completely to Him about how you've been feeling. He wants to heal those parts of you that have been weighing you down for so long.

The beauty about your suffering is that when you're in it, God feels closer than ever. In your grief, you have the opportunity to experience God's presence in a different way than you experience His presence when you're in joy. You have the opportunity to taste and see the goodness of God even in the midst of your unbearable pain.

God has brought you this far. He's taken you through hills and valleys and you've walked with Him in complete darkness. Even though things may feel darker now, God has never changed. He's allowed you to get to this place of emptiness because He has great plans in store for you and a great story of redemption He's bringing you. Stay right in His presence. Don't turn back. He's with you in all your pain and He has a plan for your recovery.

Prayer: Heavenly Father, thank you for being the safest place I could ever share my heart. Lord, I pray that if I have wounds from my past that are keeping me from being completely vulnerable with you, I pray that you would reveal those areas to me so I can bring them to you and receive healing. Help me to keep taking one step at a time with you and trusting you in the dark. I love you Lord. In Jesus name, amen.

Take Communion with the Lord.

Day 22

When?

If not now, then when?
If no change now.... then when?
Lord, I've been waiting for a long time it seems to see your hand put the puzzle pieces together.
For a while, everything has felt scattered and uncertain...
I've cried so many tears and I have experienced a lot of hurting.
If not now, then when?
If no change now...then when?

I'm doing my best to remain hopeful.
I know you're a good father and you're faithful to your word...
So, I've been clinging onto and believing in every promise I've heard.

Years have passed by and I'm still faithfully believing.
Even though there are days it feels like I can't stop weeping.
I'm trusting in you to bring the puzzle pieces together.
I'm believing for sunshiny days instead of stormy weather.
If not now, then when?

Not only have you been waiting, but the Lord has been waiting as well! He's been anticipating the moments of your life that are tied to your destiny and your calling! But he hasn't been waiting in a place of desperation because He knows what He's orchestrated and ordained over your life, He knows the timing of it, and He knows the processing you need to carry the gifts and talents He's placed inside of you.

May your waiting not be from a place of desperation but may your waiting be a place where you get to wait together with the Lord in joy, faith, and excitement. Of course there are moments where the wait has been so long that we have to ask the Lord to reignite the flame within us and to breathe life on our dry bones. But may we always redirect our hearts to the Lord when the pain becomes too much to bear.

You may be at a point in your life right now, where it seems like things couldn't become any more dead or empty...or hopeless looking. You may be feeling like, "if not now, then when?" And if that's you today, I want to remind you that those feelings of utter despair are actually signs of breakthrough coming soon. Because the Lord sees your heart. And the Lord is moved with compassion when He sees His children feeling defeated. The breakthrough that comes, may not be exactly what you've pictured to see. It may be a breakthrough that comes in a different form; based off of what the Lord knows you need right now in this moment. But I can promise you, that the Lord will come through for you! And in due time, He WILL bring the puzzle pieces of your life together.

When Mary finally found Jesus outside the village, she fell at his feet in tears and said, "Lord, if only you had been here, my brother would not have died." When Jesus looked at Mary and saw her weeping at his feet, and all her friends who were with her grieving, he shuddered with emotion and was deeply moved with tenderness and compassion.

He said to them, "Where did you bury him?" "Lord, come with us and we'll show you," they replied. Then tears streamed down Jesus' face. Seeing Jesus weep caused many of the mourners to say, "Look how much he loved Lazarus." Yet others said, "Isn't this the One who opens blind eyes? Why didn't he do something to keep Lazarus from dying?"

Then Jesus, with intense emotions, came to the tomb—a cave with a stone placed over its entrance. Jesus told them, "Roll away the stone." Then Martha said, "But Lord, it's been four days since he died—by now his body is already decomposing!" Jesus looked at her and said, "Didn't I tell you that if you will believe in me, you will see God unveil his power?"

So they rolled away the heavy stone. Jesus gazed into heaven and said, "Father, thank you that you have heard my prayer, for you listen to every word I speak. Now, so that these who stand here with me will believe that you have sent me to the earth as your messenger, I will use the power you have given me."

Then with a loud voice Jesus shouted with authority: "Lazarus!

Come out of the tomb!" Then in front of everyone, Lazarus, who had died four days earlier, slowly hobbled out—he still had grave clothes tightly wrapped around his hands and feet and covering his face! Jesus said to them, "Unwrap him and let him loose."
John 11:32-44

Prayer: Heavenly Father, you see the areas of my life where I've lost strength. There are areas in my life where I'm beginning to feel defeated. I almost feel like I'm beginning to accept defeat over my life. But I know that's a lie. God awaken my heart to your presence in these dark moments where everything feels uncertain. Awaken my senses to the signs of life that are around me. Help me to stand strong in you. Give me the patience and endurance to continue to wait with you. Help me to remember that I'm not waiting alone but that I have my savior whose waiting with me for all the great things He has in store. Thank you Father for never leaving me. Thank you for knowing the perfect timing for all things of my life. I love you Lord.
In Jesus name, amen.

Take Communion with the Lord.

Day 23

Mercy Kisses

Take me somewhere new.
Somewhere I can rest and find healing.
Somewhere I can spread my wings and fly.
I hear you saying I've been around this mountain long enough.
Create new paths for me.
Carry me into the land you've promised me.
The land where I can thrive instead of merely just survive.
The land where I can find comfort and joy in the relationships it brings.
The land where I no longer wander but where I build and establish.
Take me to this place.
You've promised me new wine and new beginnings.
You've promised to fill me up and send me out.

You've promised to give me exceedingly and abundantly more than I could ever ask or imagine.
I know there's been a process and a hefty price to pay.
But in the grand scheme of things, its nothing in comparison to what you've done for me.
Your body beaten and bruised for me to give me freedom.
Your name constantly ridiculed and spit on.
Allow me to cling tight to your goodness...knowing that what I've encountered all of these years,
is ultimately your mercy.
Your mercy and goodness and faithfulness is what is bringing me into this new land.
You've refined me and prepared me to be certain that I was ready for what you needed to place into my hands.
You've taken your time with me to shape me and mold me and make sure I was ready to be an instrument in your hands.
The waiting...all this time, has been your mercy.
So I thank you Lord, for your mercy that you've poured out over me.
And deep in my heart, I know that soon, very soon, I'll be crossing over with you into this new land you've prepared for me.

There's absolutely nothing wrong with desiring the new that the Lord has promised you. But let's be reminded daily, that ultimately nothing compares to the eternity the Lord has promised us with Him. To know that one day we'll live with our God and our Jesus, forever and evermore... is the greatest thing we get to wait upon. Nothing can measure up to the beauty of that truth.

While you're waiting, cling to the truth that your waiting is God's mercy. The Lord knows how dangerous it would be to give you anything prematurely. Be reminded that the Lord is kissing you with mercy when He has you in waiting. Celebrate with gladness that He's such a good Father and knows exactly what you need and when you need it.

Also, don't allow lies to enter your mind that would try to make you believe things will never change for you. Don't believe the lies of the enemy trying to tell you that God isn't as good as He says He is. Don't listen to the voice in your head that tells you that things were better for you before you stepped out in faith. In fact, we need to break off those lies today. As you read this, speak this out loud:

I come out of agreement with every lie I've allowed myself to believe thinking that this is all the Lord has for me. I come out of agreement with believing that things will never change. I yoke myself to the Lord's timing and His will for my life and I speak to my faith, to rise up now in the name of Jesus.

Prayer: Heavenly Father, thank you for filling me with a righteousness for your will and a submission to your timing. Thank you for kissing me with your mercy and never releasing anything to me too soon. I trust you. Forgive me for any thoughts I've had that have shown a lack of faith. Forgive me for any unbelief that's been hidden my heart. I submit myself to you and all that you have planned. Not my will be done, but yours. I love you Lord. In Jesus name, amen.

Take Communion with the Lord.

Day 24

Surprise!

Surprise!
Surprise, my child!
You thought all that pain and adversity was for nothing?
Take a look and see!
I took the most troublesome battles and forged a powerful testimony!
Look up!
The heavens are open and I'm downpouring my goodness on your land!
This new territory...it's yours.
These blessings...they're yours.
They can't be stolen. No one can take this from you.
I've placed a hedge of protection around these new blessings you're walking into.
This is your recompense!

For every battle you fought, every dark night you
faced...you've still held onto me.
You've remained faithful.
And as your heavenly Father, my nature is faithful.
I've brought you into a brand new life.
Here it is. It's yours.
It's a life filled with the promises I've been speaking over you
for years.
It's finally here.
You can shout it from the rooftops!
You can tell the world what a good Father I am!
You can tell the broken and weary that I really am who I say I
am.
You've seen it for yourself.
Give the broken the encouragement they're needing right
now. Tell them to keep clinging onto me.
Tell them that although they cannot see it yet, I'm doing
something GRAND in their life.
Tell them to remain faithful.
But also tell them, even though you're now standing in every
promise I've made to you...
That there is nothing sweeter than ME.
That the promises themselves don't even measure up to the
greatness that is found in me.
Tell them, that your promiseland has been a way for you to see
me in an even newer light!
That it's opened up the doors of revelation to who I really am
as your Father.
That when you look at your promises, all you see is ME.

All you see and think is:
"My daddy did that!"
When people ask you how you're living the life you are now,
Let your answer always be:
"My daddy did that!"
And even though what you're standing in now is mind-blowing...
You just wait and see what I've prepared for you when I return.
You haven't seen anything yet!
You just wait until you come face to face with me and get to dwell where I dwell.
Everything else pales in comparison.
My child, I am so proud of you.
Keep praising me. Keep remembering me. Keep doing my will.
A new adventure has just begun!

What a look of awe and wonder you will have on your face when you taste the fulfillment of the promises of God. There will be times in your life where you will get to experience the hand of God like you've never experienced His hand before. Much of your life has been about waiting but there is an appointed time in your life where the Lord uncovers you, launches you, and doubles your blessings.

As a warrior of God, you know what it's like to face great loss. I'm sure you've experienced seasons in your life where you've felt like you could relate to Job in the Bible. In Job, Satan had asked the Lord if He could sift Job like wheat to see if Job was truly a lover of God. Satan's method of sifting Job, was no different than how it usually is: to kill, steal, and destroy. Much like you've probably experienced yourself.

You've most likely lost a lot but you've continued to endure because you trust and love the Lord. But just like the end of Job where God doubled his blessings, you'll soon experience the same thing! There will no longer be locusts in your land attempting to destroy everything that you have! When the Lord brings you into the new, like mentioned in this poem, His hedge of protection will be around you and what He blesses you with.

Praise God for new beginnings! The Lord has you covered, and even in your great loss, **He's sustained you.** But just you wait and see the new way the Lord comes upon your life in the place of blessing He's bringing you into!

Prayer: Heavenly Father, thank you, thank you, thank you for what you have in store! Thank you that I have the faith to believe that you have great plans for me! Thank you that I have the faith to believe that the locust will no longer steal from me! Thank you that I believe that you're restoring everything the locust has stolen from me! Thank you that I'm not allowing my thoughts of the past to trick me into believing that that's all my life will ever consist of! Thank you, thank you, thank you. I love you Lord. In Jesus name, amen.

Day 25

~

From "Very Little" to "Very Much"

In the secret, I've trained you.
You've felt the crushing, the pressing, and the squeezing...
At times you've had very little...
Very little strength. Very little happiness. Very little finances.
But all those times, you had the fullness of my spirit.
My spirit has empowered you in your weakest of moments.
And you know this.
You've learned what it's like to live with a little. Not just a little, VERY little.
You've seen my spirit move in the little, now it's time for you to see my spirit move in the abundance.
No longer will you stand in "very little."
It's time for you to flourish in "very much."

Just as you sought me in “very little”, you will seek me in “very much.”

You’ve been prepared for this.

I can trust you with this.

You’re my warrior child.

Your hands have been trained to war, your mind has been trained to overcome, and your heart has been purified to remain humble.

You’re ready.

Keep me at the forefront of your mind.

Let everything you do, be done in my name.

Don’t step outside of my will.

It’s my pleasure to give you the kingdom.

And as you keep giving me your heart, I’ll keep revealing more of my kingdom to you.

The best is yet to come.

You've been empowered by the Lord to take the land! You've been prepared by God to enter into "very much." Your heart needed to be emptied, refined, and humbled to grasp onto all that the Lord has for you. He's been preparing a moment for His glory to be showcased to all those around you. Praise God for "very little!" Even in your "very little," you had "very much" because you had your Heavenly Father. But just you wait! Wait until you see what the Lord does with your "very little" and how His mighty arm moves on your behalf. Stay steadfast in His love. For all the places the Lord takes you, no matter how small or how large, great impact will be made. His spirit is strong in you and He has made you ready to be a carrier of His word.

Prayer: Heavenly Father, I pray that I am a good steward of all that you place in my hands. I thank you for leading me so gently into these new places. I thank you for taking care of my heart and preparing me to be a good steward over everything you desire that I walk in. You are my prize and I love you. Thank you for your spirit, and your truth, and your love.
In Jesus name, amen.

Take Communion with the Lord.

Day 26

You are a Conqueror

Case Closed!
The accuser will not prevail against you.
The battle is yours.
With the blood of the Lamb and the word of your testimony,
you will conquer the wicked one.
When you rise up in your authority and open up your mouth,
every wicked agenda against you must crumble.
Every demonic agent must leave you.
I've given you the authority to trample on serpents and
scorpions.
The sting of the enemy has been defeated by my blood!
There is no reason for you to lay with your head between your
knees.
There is no reason for you to hide.

There is no reason for you to cower like a frightened dog with its tail between its legs.
The victory is yours!
I want you to proclaim it!
Take what I have given you and use your voice!
Speak my truth over any wicked lie that attempts to attack your mind.
Fix your posture and know who you are!
You are a Child of God. You are a Warrior of God.
You are a Royal Priesthood.
The Kingdom is yours.
Be not afraid, go forth in courage!
I've given you the authority to take dominion!
Take dominion over every opposing force that rises up against you!
Watch every giant fall as you stand on my name and testify to WHO I AM.
They're no match for you.

It is time to open up your mouth! After years of suffering, it can be easy to begin to clam up. If you've been in isolation for a while, sometimes you've gotten used to the silence and quietness. But it's time to make some noise for the Kingdom of God. It's no longer time to be a bystander. It's time to rise up and proclaim the gospel! It's time to rise up and speak against the voice of the accuser. It's time to rise up and let truth ring! It's time for the "sound of freedom" to be released from the depths of your bones! **You were created for this.** You were created to minister the truth, the love, and the freedom of the gospel. You were created to preach reconciliation to all those you encounter. And you were created to trample on the serpents head and walk victoriously as an overcomer and an Heir of God. Take back your position of authority and ARISE.

You. Are. A. Conqueror.

Prayer: Heavenly Father, praise you God. Praise you King of Kings. Thank you for your overwhelming love that causes me to act! Thank you for bubbling up a deep passion within me to where I am bursting at the seams! Thank you that I am ready to explode for your Kingdom. Thank you that I am an overcomer in you and I am an unstoppable force. Praise you King Jesus! Thank you for your blood and your body! Thank you for your power! Thank you for the power of your spirit flowing through me. Thank you for gracing me with new gifts of the spirit. I love you Lord. I trust you God. I know that you are for me and where you send me, I will go. Thank you for filling me up with the spirit of boldness so I always speak what you need me to speak. I will no longer care what others think of me but I will step into void places and release the power of God to let it fill up those spaces with TRUTH! I will no longer be held back or shut up by the enemy. I am going to let my voice ring forth. Thank you for the voice you've given me. Praise you God!

In Jesus name, amen.

Take Communion with the Lord.

Day 27

Here

Should you ever feel you need to rest,
do just that, and take a deep breath.
Lean into me and pursue my spirit.
Follow my voice, you will certainly hear it.
My yoke is easy and my burden is light.
Come and rest under me,
there are no worries in sight.
In me, you'll find peace and rest for your soul.
I'm the best leader when you relinquish control.
You can trust that I'll lead you in the everlasting way.
My word is my word, yes, I mean what I say.
When I say I'll never leave, that's exactly what I mean.
When I tell you I am trustworthy, there is no in between.
I know you've been tired and you've been weary from it all,

but cast your cares and anxiety onto me and watch every burden fall.
This battle isn't to the swift nor is it to the strong.
Just put your trust in me and watch me right every wrong.
With quiet confidence and humility, you'll go further than the rest.
Stay hidden under me and remember that I always know best.
My ways and thoughts are higher, higher than your own understanding.
You've been trying to plan your own way, but I've already done all the planning.
There's no need to be in a panic or to think you need all the answers now.
In my absolute perfect timing, I'll give you the directions and I'll show you how!
The only thing I need from you is for you to keep lingering in my presence.
So come and drink from my living waters and be overcome with my essence.
I am abounding in love and I am mindful of your humanity.
So when you question me because you don't understand, I listen to your questions patiently.
At the right time I will answer...
and it may not be how you think.
But I promise you when I come with answers, it will be everything you need!
I know what I am doing and I know the destiny I've placed inside of you!

I have no intentions to harm you, I only have good plans for you!
I've begun a good work in you and I will certainly bring it into completion.
And as you continue to rest in me, I'll teach you how to walk in each season.
Keep taking deep breaths and remain sheltered under my wings.
I will always be your safe place and will tell you great and incomprehensible things.
In the secret place there's no hurry, there's no hustle, and there's no rush.
You will only find my peace and a tangible holy hush.
In the waiting, you'll be resting... and in the quiet, your ears are inclined to hear...
my ever loving, still, small voice, reminding you.... "I AM HERE!"

At the right time He will answer! We can be quick to become impatient and feel like we need answers right away. But when we step into the Lord and we're in the rivers of His Kingdom, we will find that the pace of the Kingdom is much different than the ways of the world. Sometimes we must remind our souls to slow down and to find peace in God's presence. We don't have to be in a hurry and we can trust that if we don't have the answers in the very moment we think we need them, that we don't actually need them in that very second. We have to rely on knowing that God is our Shepherd and such a good Father, that in his perfect timing

He will release all the solutions and directions we are needing. So let this be your reminder today, to slow down. To remind yourself that the Lord has everything under control. He hasn't left you. The silence is there to linger with Him and wait on Him. Continue in the waiting. The Lord will release what you need, when you need it. Remain in trust.

Prayer: Heavenly Father, guard me from taking things into my own hands. Increase my patience and trust in you. Help me to remember that you have everything under control. I know that my heart is submitted to you, therefore I can know that I am in your will and that you are the one who will "cause" things to happen in my life. Help me to remember that sometimes, all I need to do is just wait a little longer and trust! Just because things aren't moving yet, doesn't mean that they're not going to move. Just because answers haven't arrived yet, doesn't mean answers aren't coming. Just because I think I need change right now, doesn't mean I need it in this very moment. Help me to remember and know, that YOU know what's best for me. And I can trust in that. Thank you Lord. I love you.

In Jesus name, amen.

Take Communion with the Lord.

Day 28

The Way

Feast on me.
In your weariness and in your waiting...
When you're hungry for change...
Feast on me.
I do not give as the world gives.
I do not come to fill you up, only to leave you feeling empty.
I come to fill you up to overflowing. Always leaving you satisfied.
I am the only one who can supply you with your every need.
In this place where you're so desperately desiring a different way,
You can always enter into my presence and be mesmerized by THE WAY.
My presence brings peace when you feel surrounded by chaos.

My love brings healing when you feel overwhelmed with pain
My wisdom brings clarity when you feel clouded with uncertainty.
My power brings strength when you feel unbearably weak.
I am THE WAY.
I am what you can always partake of.
I know you're hungry.
I know you're thirsty.
But child, let your desperation be for me and for me alone.
You know I will make all things right and you can rest in that.
Turn your focus to longing for more of me.
I want to show you THE WAY.

Open your eyes son/daughter. There is a way set before you. It is THE WAY. Jesus. He is looking at you with eyes of fire that pierce your soul with the deepest love you've ever experienced. With Him in your line of sight, you will be mesmerized. You will be taken over by so much love that your deepest desire will be to follow His call, no matter what the cost. Lay it all down and follow THE WAY. He's beckoning you. He's drawing you into more of Him. More of the Kingdom. Come and feast on THE WAY.

Prayer: Heavenly Father, bring me to my knees in you. Bring me to a beautiful surrender. Let my eyes lock with yours. Have me so undone in your presence that the only thing I desire is to do your will. Fill me with a passion that moves me to move in the way that you do. Satisfy the cravings of my soul. Help me to step outside of the soulish realm and step into the realm of the Kingdom. Your realm

of glory. I know that in you, I will never thirst or hunger for the things of this world. Thank you Lord.
In Jesus name, amen.

Take Communion with the Lord.

Day 29

Come Up Higher

A crowded mind struggles to find me...
It's crowded with social media,
crowded with worries about tomorrow,
and crowded with anxiety...

To the busy mind I say:
"Come up higher and get out of your head.

Tune in to
Rest.
Understand I Am
Safety and...
Trust me.

Do not worry about tomorrow,
For tomorrow will worry about itself.
Do not compare your life to theirs,
You have much to be grateful for.
Come up higher and get out of your head.

I want to show you a
New perspective...the Kingdom perspective.

Taste and see that I am good.
Fix your eyes on the cross and the freedom I've already given you.
Look back on your life and see where I've brought you.
My hands are on everything.
My eyes are on you always.
You are not forgotten.
You have been reserved.
So come up higher and get out of your head.

Mighty Warrior...
Enter into my rest. "

You're entering into new heights, Kingdom Warrior! The Lord is strengthening the areas of your heart and your mind that have felt weary for so long. In the place of weariness, we can find ourselves getting accustomed to numbing the pain through keeping our minds distracted with things that stimulate our mind. But the Lord is calling out for a "Holy Hush." He's calling out for your full attention. "Come up higher!" He says. Enter into His rest. He is calling you from His Heavenly place to lay down the distractions, get out of your thoughts, and enter into His Kingdom realm. He has new things to show you and tell you. Step away from what has been distracting you and direct your eyes to Jesus. Healing is in Him. Truth is in Him. Answers are in Him.

Prayer: Heavenly Father, thank you for lifting me out of my distracted mind and bringing me up higher in you. I want to ascend the mountain with you. You are my only resting place. Hush my mind and bring my full attention to you. I want to know you more. Thank you for fixing my focus and for strengthening me. I love you.

In Jesus name, amen.

Take Communion with the Lord.

Day 30

Your Return

It's returning.
Your peace and your joy...they're returning.
The prodigals you love...they're returning.
What the enemy stole from you...it's returning.

But it's not coming back the same.
What you're about to hold in your hands... is something that your eyes haven't had a chance to see.
There's new life in what's being returned to you.
I've breathed my own breath into everything I'm releasing unto you.
It's all filled with the wind of my spirit and the rivers of my love.
It's filled with a fire that never goes out.
It's been touched by my own hand.

It's been sealed with my spirit.
I have set my lock of love on everything I'm entrusting to you.
There is no entryway for the destroyer to attempt to trespass and destroy.
You will not find ravenous beasts surrounding you when you look to the left or to the right.
You can lie down in safety.

For what came upon you in the past to torment you,
I have set my gavel on.
I have sent destruction to every enemy that has attempted to gain access to you.
The giants you once saw, you will never see again.
I have sent forth my word to do what it's meant to accomplish.
Justice has arrived and retribution is here.

It's yours.
It's finally yours.
My faithful warrior.
My good steward.

For every loss you've endured, I have multiplied your returns.
Sing praises unto me.
Not only did you withstand the fiery furnace, but you've come out ten times stronger.
You've come out 1000 times blessed.
And you've come out filled with the power of my spirit.
Take heed to the command that I give you today:

To love the Lord, your God with all your heart, with all your soul, and with all your strength.
From this day on, you will no longer be called "forsaken" or "desolate"...but your land will be called "My Delight is in Her" and your land will be married.

Things are changing for you, warrior! Lift up your eyes and see where your help comes from! Your help comes from the Lord. Speak out loud in faith today that God's promises are yes and amen! He is coming to rescue you and bless you more than before. Things won't be the same!

Robbers (Satan's agents) won't lurk around every corner seeking to devour everything your hands touch! **You're entering into a place of divine safety.** God is releasing what has been stored up for you in His perfect timing. He has been preparing this moment for you to receive your rewards. Not only does He have rewards stored up for you in Heaven for your obedience, He has rewards ordained for you to receive here on Earth. But the greatest reward you have- is His presence. He is with you where ever you go, Warrior. You no longer have to fear. The Lord has chosen you and set you apart. He is doing something new in you and through you. Keep yielding to His instructions. For where He goes, you shall follow. He's taking you to a broad place. A land of milk and honey. Taste and see.

Prayer: Heavenly Father, bless you Lord. I don't have the words to explain my love for you. You have never forsaken me. You have never abandoned me. You have never lied to me. You have kept me.

All these years, you have kept me. I couldn't be more thankful for your keeping. I love you so much Lord and I pray that everything that I do is pleasing to you. Help me to obey and follow your spirit where ever it goes. Thank you God for the blessings you're bringing me. Help me to steward them well. I trust and believe that you have good things in store for me. But never let my heart desire your gifts more than I desire your presence. Keep me on fire for your presence more than anything in this world. Never allow my heart to be swayed away from you being my number one. If there are areas in my heart where I have made anything an idol, I repent right now and I ask that you would remove every idol hiding in my heart. I shall have no other gods before you. You are the one and only true God. I love you. I love you. I love you.

In Jesus name, amen.

Take Communion with the Lord.

Day 31

In the Nick of Time

Just in the nick of time.
You came.
I had begun to feel that parts of me had given up.
I almost came to believe that things would never change.
I was close to thinking I would always live life this way.
I have been wondering "when will it ever get good?"
But it's just like you, my God, to come just in the nick of time.

Some would say they'd never believe you to just show up so out of the blue.
When chances for change look awfully slim and the options have ran out for things to do.
But much like the miracle worker that you've always been, you come in and turn things around right on time.

After things have been dead for so long now and everything's
been constrained, you turn it around on a dime!

How unexpected, after feeling so neglected...
although that wasn't the case at all.
As I felt left to myself and felt my promises on the shelf, you
were constructing a plan and a way for it all.
I had begun to get angry and kept asking you to save me...I
didn't want to feel resentment at all.
What a good Father, to hear the words of His daughter, and
capture every emotion that would attempt to make her fall.
Right when I thought it was over, you rushed in much closer,
with a plan for longings fulfilled.
You spoke to me kindly and you stood right behind me, with
directions to follow your call.

I heeded to your promptings, remained steadfast to my
commitments, and loved you with my whole heart and my soul.
I sat back while you directed, then followed the steps you
commanded, and watched how you took control.
You've turned my mourning to dancing and my sorrow to
laughter...I'm made new by this refreshing...I'll never be the same.
I've been refined by your fire and I've been crushed in the
waiting...I'll forever be proclaiming your name!

I'll let every believer know to never stop trusting no matter
how dark and directionless everything may feel.
I'll tell them to keep holding on, and never stop believing,
because all that their Father has promised them is real!

I'll remind them that things may get darker before they get
brighter but to remain steadfast at their Fathers feet.
Because just in the nick of time, their Father will come, and
He always brings victory to the meek!

Your victory is in Jesus!!! He always comes right on time, even when it looks like it's too late to us, it's perfect timing for His plans!!! Because of every dark day you've encountered and every battle you've faced, you now carry a message that will bring hope to many people you'll meet over the course of your life! God is going to make things right for you! You won't always live life in survival mode or in a place of grief. A new day is promised to you, from your Heavenly Father.

Continue walking in His light and heeding to His every command. You will be exactly where you need to be and everything will be going according to plan, as long as you continue to remain at His feet. The Lord, your God, is a good Father. He's a good Shepherd. And oh, is He faithful! Not one promise He has made to you will fall void. Cling to His presence and fix your eyes on His face, and you could never go wrong! Be strengthened today by the simple fact that God is who He say's He is and that will NEVER change.

What is mankind that you are mindful of them, human beings that you care for them? You have made them a little lower than the angels and crowned them with glory and honor. You made them rulers over the works of your hands; you put everything under their

feet: all flocks and herds, and the animals of the wild, the birds in the sky, and the fish in the sea, all that swim the paths of the seas. Lord, our Lord, how majestic is your name in all the earth!
Psalms 8:4-9

Therefore I tell you, do not be anxious about your life, what you will eat or what you will drink, nor about your body, what you will put on. Is not life more than food, and the body more than clothing? Look at the birds of the air: they neither sow nor reap nor gather into barns, and yet your heavenly Father feeds them. Are you not of more value than they? And which of you by being anxious can add a single hour to his span of life?
Matthew 6:25-27

God's eyes are on you. And everything is going according to plan.

Prayer: Heavenly Father, thank you for holding me in your hands. Thank you for the breakthroughs you have in store for me. Thank you for tearing down any prison walls that have surrounded me. I thank you for the strength you've given me and the new-found freedom I get to walk in. Thank you that you've given me a message that will help so many people! Thank you that every single one of your promises will be fulfilled in my life! I love you, I love you, I love you.
In Jesus name, amen.

Take Communion with the Lord.

Alex Blackburn has a heart desire to see people walking in complete freedom and living life at their fullest potential. Through her writing, speaking, and music, her goal is to point people to Jesus, bring their hearts encouragement, and aid in their transformation. Alex resides in North Carolina, with her daughter, Maliyah.

Connect with Alex by visiting www.alexchristianministries.com

www.ingramcontent.com/pod-product-compliance
Ingram Content Group UK Ltd.
Pitfield, Milton Keynes, MK11 3LW, UK
UKHW042002190726
13854UKWH00005B/2133